Peter W. Wielhouwer, Ph.D.

Study Guide for American National Government (2020-22)

For use with American Government, 2nd Edition, by Timothy O. Lenz and Mirya Holman (University Press of Florida, 2018)

ISBN: 9781661830380

© 2020 Peter Warren Wielhouwer

Study Guide for American National Government

Table of Contents

(Note: Textbook chapters are in the order in which I typically assign them for my class)

Introduction 1

How to study the textbook using this Study Guide 3

The Declaration of Independence 7

The United States Constitution 11

Chapter 1. Why Government? Why Politics? 29

Chapter 2. The U.S. System of Constitutional Government 31

Chapter 6. Federalism 33

Chapter 16. Civil Liberties and Civil Rights 35

Chapter 8. Public Opinion 37

Chapter 9. Political Ideology 39

OpenStax American Government, Chapter 7. Voting and Elections 41

Chapter 10. Political Participation 43

Chapter 11. Political Parties 45

Chapter 12. Interest Groups 47

Chapter 7. The Media, Politics, and Government 49

Chapter 3. Congress 51

Chapter 4. The Presidency 53

Chapter 5. The Courts 55

Chapter 13. Public Policy 57

Introduction

I have designed this Study Guide to help students organize and study from the course material used in the American government textbook *American Government*, 2nd Edition, by Timothy O. Lenz and Mirya Holman. The Lenz and Holman textbook is available free of charge for download at http://ufdc.ufl.edu/AA00061950/00001.

I have organized the sequence of chapters in this guide according to the order in which I normally teach the chapter content in my classes, which is different from the order in which the textbook orders the content.

In creating this guide, I build on years of experience in education to provide suggested learning activities for students to best learn and comprehend the textbook material. While most chapters in the textbook have study questions and vocabulary lists written by the text authors, I have created my own set of study questions that reflects my reading of the text and its organization. There is, of course, some overlap, but I provided my pilot study questions for a few chapters to my Fall 2019 American Government class, and students remarked that they found my questions to be more helpful in studying the text material.

For each topic, chapter, or reading there are several suggested learning activities that will help students learn and reinforce the material in the readings. I have formatted these activities with check boxes (❏) to help students track completion of the learning activities. I recognize that different people have different learning styles, so students should pick and choose the learning activities that best fit your own situation. While those choices are up to you, I recommend that you use a variety of them to best learn and retain the course content. The recommended learning activities are adapted from the **SQ3R** study strategy. In this strategy, a student will

- **Survey** the assigned reading, in order to get a preview of what the author's main points are and how the chapter is organized. Next, the student will
- **Question** the reading, by forming some initial questions about the chapter content based on their initial survey and their own interests, beliefs, and experiences. Questioning helps students read the chapter with purpose (that is, to find answers to these questions). Next, the student will
- **Read** the chapter carefully and purposefully. Finally,
- **Review** the material in the chapter (through learning activities such as flashcards, the textbook's website resources, and through personally outlining each chapter).

In the next section, I suggest a plan for using the Study Guide to help students learn and retain the material effectively.

Finally, please do not provide copies of this study guide to others...I've spent many hours developing it, and pirating copies is illegal under United States copyright law.

I welcome your feedback on the aspects of this Study Guide that you find helpful, and those that you do not find helpful. This information will help me to improve this product for future students.

Best wishes,

Dr. Peter W. Wielhouwer

Kalamazoo, Michigan, 2020

How to study the textbook using this Study Guide

Learning course material well requires time and effort; my goal in this section is to give you a plan and strategy for effective use of your time. While these are not the only methods of studying, using some or all of these recommendations will help you learn and retain the course material well, enabling you to approach assessments and classes with confidence.

Overview

Begin studying each chapter using the first several learning activities in the respective Study Guide chapter.

First, SURVEY the chapter.

- ❑ Read the introductory paragraphs at the beginning of the chapter.
- ❑ Read the "Summary" paragraphs at the end of the chapter.
- ❑ Scan the chapter, noting the major headings and subheadings, and bolded vocabulary terms
- ❑ Take note of tables and figures in the chapter.

Second, QUESTION the material in the chapter.

- ❑ Based on your survey of the major headings and subheadings of the chapter, generate a set of your own questions about the chapter.
- ❑ Review the study questions in this guide for the chapter, and note how they correspond to the major sections of the chapter.

Next, systematically READ the chapter.

- ❑ Read the chapter carefully in light of the study guide questions and the questions you have developed.
- ❑ Outline the chapter, noting key concepts and the authors' conclusions.
- ❑ Make flashcards for the vocabulary terms and key concepts.
- ❑ Take advantage of the hotlinks provided in the digital version of the chapter to expand your understanding of the chapter content.

Finally, REVIEW the chapter and your notes as you move toward assessments (such as quizzes or tests).

- ❑ Review the study guide questions and your own study questions, attempting to address those questions in your own words.
- ❑ Review your own notes

Taking notes on the reading

Once you've surveyed a reading selection (the first set of boxes listed above), here is how you might outline a chapter based on the Study Guide. Let's look at Chapter 8 on Public Opinion 8 (specifically, pages 190-193) for a brief example.

In the Study Guide section on chapter 8 the initial study questions are:

1. How does "public opinion" pertain to the power problem? How do the two major models of democratic systems view public opinion? What are presidential approval ratings and what affects them? What does it mean to "wag the dog"?
2. What is "public opinion"? What is the Delegate Model? What is the Trustee Model? What were the Founders' Intentions with regard to public opinion?

Note that these question numbers correspond to the major section numbers in the chapter. Note also that the text authors have divided the content by "chunks" or subsections to help you organize your time and reading.

To create your own study notes, begin with the first question, find the main points in the text that answer the question, and <u>briefly</u> write in your own words the main points. Your notes might then look something like this (page, paragraph or section references are on the right so you can see where I got the information).

1. How does "public opinion" pertain to the power problem?	Text
-Whether PO is a cause of public policy or is caused to change by public policy	p. 190, ¶ 2
-Democratic theory says PO should influence policy (Classical Democratic Systems model)	
-But PO is dynamic	
1a. How do the two major models of democratic systems view public opinion?	
- Classical Dem Systems	p. 193, ¶ 2-3
- Modified Dem System: campaigns and media are designed to change PO, so PO both affects policy and is affected by what people learn.	
1b. What are presidential approval ratings and what affects them?	p. 194, section 8.11
-measures of public opinion about how the president is doing.	
-affected by the economy, important events, "rally around the flag" effect (like 9/11)	
1b. What does it mean to "wag the dog"?	p. 194-195, section 8.1
-presidents might create a military emergency to distract the public from problems.	

By systematically and strategically reading in this way, your mind processes information in multiple ways, improving your learning and memory by integrating cognitive processes involved in previewing, preparing and organizing, reading, highlighting or underlining important information and definitions, summarizing, putting things in your own words, physically writing things down, and comparing what you wrote with what is in the text, and reviewing your own notes all are important parts of the strategic studying process.

The Declaration of Independence

In Congress, July 4, 1776.

The unanimous Declaration of the thirteen united States of America, When in the Course of human events, it becomes necessary for one people to dissolve the political bands which have connected them with another, and to assume among the powers of the earth, the separate and equal station to which the Laws of Nature and of Nature's God entitle them, a decent respect to the opinions of mankind requires that they should declare the causes which impel them to the separation.

We hold these truths to be self-evident, that all men are created equal, that they are endowed by their Creator with certain unalienable Rights, that among these are Life, Liberty and the pursuit of Happiness.--That to secure these rights, Governments are instituted among Men, deriving their just powers from the consent of the governed, --That whenever any Form of Government becomes destructive of these ends, it is the Right of the People to alter or to abolish it, and to institute new Government, laying its foundation on such principles and organizing its powers in such form, as to them shall seem most likely to effect their Safety and Happiness. Prudence, indeed, will dictate that Governments long established should not be changed for light and transient causes; and accordingly all experience hath shewn, that mankind are more disposed to suffer, while evils are sufferable, than to right themselves by abolishing the forms to which they are accustomed. But when a long train of abuses and usurpations, pursuing invariably the same Object evinces a design to reduce them under absolute Despotism, it is their right, it is their duty, to throw off such Government, and to provide new Guards for their future security.--Such has been the patient sufferance of these Colonies; and such is now the necessity which constrains them to alter their former Systems of Government. The history of the present King of Great Britain is a history of repeated injuries and usurpations, all having in direct object the establishment of an absolute Tyranny over these States. To prove this, let Facts be submitted to a candid world.

He has refused his Assent to Laws, the most wholesome and necessary for the public good.

He has forbidden his Governors to pass Laws of immediate and pressing importance, unless suspended in their operation till his Assent should be obtained; and when so suspended, he has utterly neglected to attend to them.

He has refused to pass other Laws for the accommodation of large districts of people, unless those people would relinquish the right of Representation in the Legislature, a right inestimable to them and formidable to tyrants only.

He has called together legislative bodies at places unusual, uncomfortable, and distant from the depository of their public Records, for the sole purpose of fatiguing them into compliance with his measures.

He has dissolved Representative Houses repeatedly, for opposing with manly firmness his invasions on the rights of the people.

He has refused for a long time, after such dissolutions, to cause others to be elected; whereby the Legislative powers, incapable of Annihilation, have returned to the People at large for their exercise; the State remaining in the mean time exposed to all the dangers of invasion from without, and convulsions within.

He has endeavoured to prevent the population of these States; for that purpose obstructing the Laws for Naturalization of Foreigners; refusing to pass others to encourage their migrations hither, and raising the conditions of new Appropriations of Lands.

He has obstructed the Administration of Justice, by refusing his Assent to Laws for establishing Judiciary powers.

He has made Judges dependent on his Will alone, for the tenure of their offices, and the amount and payment of their salaries.

He has erected a multitude of New Offices, and sent hither swarms of Officers to harrass our people, and eat out their substance.

He has kept among us, in times of peace, Standing Armies without the Consent of our legislatures.

He has affected to render the Military independent of and superior to the Civil power.

He has combined with others to subject us to a jurisdiction foreign to our constitution, and unacknowledged by our laws; giving his Assent to their Acts of pretended Legislation:

For Quartering large bodies of armed troops among us:

For protecting them, by a mock Trial, from punishment for any Murders which they should commit on the Inhabitants of these States:

For cutting off our Trade with all parts of the world:

For imposing Taxes on us without our Consent:

For depriving us in many cases, of the benefits of Trial by Jury:

For transporting us beyond Seas to be tried for pretended offences

For abolishing the free System of English Laws in a neighbouring Province, establishing therein an Arbitrary government, and enlarging its Boundaries so as to render it at once an example and fit instrument for introducing the same absolute rule into these Colonies:

For taking away our Charters, abolishing our most valuable Laws, and altering fundamentally the Forms of our Governments:

For suspending our own Legislatures, and declaring themselves invested with power to legislate for us in all cases whatsoever.

He has abdicated Government here, by declaring us out of his Protection and waging War against us.

He has plundered our seas, ravaged our Coasts, burnt our towns, and destroyed the lives of our people.

He is at this time transporting large Armies of foreign Mercenaries to compleat the works of death, desolation and tyranny, already begun with circumstances of Cruelty & perfidy scarcely paralleled in the most barbarous ages, and totally unworthy the Head of a civilized nation.

He has constrained our fellow Citizens taken Captive on the high Seas to bear Arms against their Country, to become the executioners of their friends and Brethren, or to fall themselves by their Hands.

He has excited domestic insurrections amongst us, and has endeavoured to bring on the inhabitants of our frontiers, the merciless Indian Savages, whose known rule of warfare, is an undistinguished destruction of all ages, sexes and conditions.

In every stage of these Oppressions We have Petitioned for Redress in the most humble terms: Our repeated Petitions have been answered only by repeated injury. A Prince whose character is thus marked by every act which may define a Tyrant, is unfit to be the ruler of a free people.

Nor have We been wanting in attentions to our Brittish brethren. We have warned them from time to time of attempts by their legislature to extend an unwarrantable jurisdiction over us. We have reminded them of the circumstances of our emigration and settlement here. We have appealed to their native justice and magnanimity, and we have conjured them by the ties of our common kindred to disavow these usurpations, which, would inevitably interrupt our connections and correspondence. They too have been deaf to the voice of justice and of consanguinity. We must, therefore, acquiesce in the necessity, which denounces our Separation, and hold them, as we hold the rest of mankind, Enemies in War, in Peace Friends.

We, therefore, the Representatives of the united States of America, in General Congress, Assembled, appealing to the Supreme Judge of the world for the rectitude of our intentions, do, in the Name, and by Authority of the good People of these Colonies, solemnly publish and declare, That these United Colonies are, and of Right ought to be Free and Independent States; that they are Absolved from all Allegiance to the British Crown, and that all political connection between them and the State of Great Britain, is and ought to be totally dissolved; and that as Free and Independent States, they have full Power to levy War, conclude Peace, contract Alliances, establish Commerce, and to do all other Acts and Things which Independent States may of right do. And for the support of this Declaration, with a firm reliance on the protection of divine Providence, we mutually pledge to each other our Lives, our Fortunes and our sacred Honor.

Georgia	Maryland	Delaware	Massachusetts
Button Gwinnett	Samuel Chase	Caesar Rodney	Samuel Adams
Lyman Hall	William Paca	George Read	John Adams
George Walton	Thomas Stone	Thomas McKean	Robert Treat Paine
	Charles Carroll of Carrollton		Elbridge Gerry
North Carolina		**New York**	
William Hooper	**Virginia**	William Floyd	**Rhode Island**

Joseph Hewes
John Penn

South Carolina
Edward Rutledge
Thomas Heyward, Jr.
Thomas Lynch, Jr.
Arthur Middleton

Massachusetts
John Hancock

George Wythe
Richard Henry Lee
Thomas Jefferson
Benjamin Harrison
Thomas Nelson, Jr.
Francis Lightfoot Lee
Carter Braxton

Pennsylvania
Robert Morris
Benjamin Rush
Benjamin Franklin
John Morton
George Clymer
James Smith
George Taylor
James Wilson
George Ross

Philip Livingston
Francis Lewis
Lewis Morris

New Jersey
Richard Stockton
John Witherspoon
Francis Hopkinson
John Hart
Abraham Clark

New Hampshire
Josiah Bartlett
William Whipple

Stephen Hopkins
William Ellery

Connecticut
Roger Sherman
Samuel Huntington
William Williams
Oliver Wolcott

New Hampshire
Matthew Thornton

Text source: "Declaration of Independence: A Transcription," 1 Nov. 2015, www.archives.gov/founding-docs/declaration-transcript.

The United States Constitution

We the People of the United States, in Order to form a more perfect Union, establish Justice, insure domestic Tranquility, provide for the common defence, promote the general Welfare, and secure the Blessings of Liberty to ourselves and our Posterity, do ordain and establish this Constitution for the United States of America.

Article I [Legislative Power: Congress]

Section 1

All legislative Powers herein granted shall be vested in a Congress of the United States, which shall consist of a Senate and House of Representatives.

Section 2

1: The House of Representatives shall be composed of Members chosen every second Year by the People of the several States, and the Electors in each State shall have the Qualifications requisite for Electors of the most numerous Branch of the State Legislature.

2: No Person shall be a Representative who shall not have attained to the Age of twenty five Years, and been seven Years a Citizen of the United States, and who shall not, when elected, be an Inhabitant of that State in which he shall be chosen.

3: *Representatives and direct Taxes shall be apportioned among the several States which may be included within this Union, according to their respective Numbers, which shall be determined by adding to the whole Number of free Persons, including those bound to Service for a Term of Years, and excluding Indians not taxed, three fifths of all other Persons.*[1] The actual Enumeration shall be made within three Years after the first Meeting of the Congress of the United States, and within every subsequent Term of ten Years, in such Manner as they shall by Law direct. The Number of Representatives shall not exceed one for every thirty Thousand, but each State shall have at Least one Representative; and until such enumeration shall be made, the State of New Hampshire shall be entitled to chuse three, Massachusetts eight, Rhode-Island and Providence Plantations one, Connecticut five, New-York six, New Jersey four, Pennsylvania eight, Delaware one, Maryland six, Virginia ten, North Carolina five, South Carolina five, and Georgia three.

4: When vacancies happen in the Representation from any State, the Executive Authority thereof shall issue Writs of Election to fill such Vacancies.

5: The House of Representatives shall chuse their Speaker and other Officers; and shall have the sole Power of Impeachment.

Section 3

---

[1] The part of Article 1 Section 2 Clause 3 relating to the mode of apportionment of representatives among the several States has been affected by Amendment XIV Section 2, and as to taxes on incomes without apportionment by Amendment XVI.

1: The Senate of the United States shall be composed of two Senators from each State, *chosen by the Legislature thereof*,[2] for six Years; and each Senator shall have one Vote.

2: Immediately after they shall be assembled in Consequence of the first Election, they shall be divided as equally as may be into three Classes. The Seats of the Senators of the first Class shall be vacated at the Expiration of the second Year, of the second Class at the Expiration of the fourth Year, and of the third Class at the Expiration of the sixth Year, so that one third may be chosen every second Year; *and if Vacancies happen by Resignation, or otherwise, during the Recess of the Legislature of any State, the Executive thereof may make temporary Appointments until the next Meeting of the Legislature, which shall then fill such Vacancies.*[3]

3: No Person shall be a Senator who shall not have attained to the Age of thirty Years, and been nine Years a Citizen of the United States, and who shall not, when elected, be an Inhabitant of that State for which he shall be chosen.

4: The Vice President of the United States shall be President of the Senate, but shall have no Vote, unless they be equally divided.

5: The Senate shall chuse their other Officers, and also a President pro tempore, in the Absence of the Vice President, or when he shall exercise the Office of President of the United States.

6: The Senate shall have the sole Power to try all Impeachments. When sitting for that Purpose, they shall be on Oath or Affirmation. When the President of the United States is tried, the Chief Justice shall preside: And no Person shall be convicted without the Concurrence of two thirds of the Members present.

7: Judgment in Cases of impeachment shall not extend further than to removal from Office, and disqualification to hold and enjoy any Office of honor, Trust or Profit under the United States: but the Party convicted shall nevertheless be liable and subject to Indictment, Trial, Judgment and Punishment, according to Law.

Section 4

1: The Times, Places and Manner of holding Elections for Senators and Representatives, shall be prescribed in each State by the Legislature thereof; but the Congress may at any time by Law make or alter such Regulations, except as to the Places of chusing Senators.

2: The Congress shall assemble at least once in every Year, and such Meeting shall be on *the first Monday in December*,[4] unless they shall by Law appoint a different Day.

Section 5

1: Each House shall be the Judge of the Elections, Returns and Qualifications of its own Members, and a Majority of each shall constitute a Quorum to do Business; but a smaller Number may adjourn from day to day, and may be authorized to compel the Attendance of absent Members, in such Manner, and under such Penalties as each House may provide.

---

[2] Article 1 Section 3 Clause 1 has been affected by Amendment XVII Section 1.
[3] Article 1 Section 3 Clause 2 has been affected by Amendment XVII Section 2.
[4] Article 1 Section 4 Clause 2 has been affected by Amendment XX.

2: Each House may determine the Rules of its Proceedings, punish its Members for disorderly Behaviour, and, with the Concurrence of two thirds, expel a Member.

3: Each House shall keep a Journal of its Proceedings, and from time to time publish the same, excepting such Parts as may in their Judgment require Secrecy; and the Yeas and Nays of the Members of either House on any question shall, at the Desire of one fifth of those Present, be entered on the Journal.

4: Neither House, during the Session of Congress, shall, without the Consent of the other, adjourn for more than three days, nor to any other Place than that in which the two Houses shall be sitting.

Section 6

1: The Senators and Representatives shall receive a Compensation for their Services, *to be ascertained by Law, and paid out of the Treasury of the United States.*[5] They shall in all Cases, except Treason, Felony and Breach of the Peace, be privileged from Arrest during their Attendance at the Session of their respective Houses, and in going to and returning from the same; and for any Speech or Debate in either House, they shall not be questioned in any other Place.

2: No Senator or Representative shall, during the Time for which he was elected, be appointed to any civil Office under the Authority of the United States, which shall have been created, or the Emoluments whereof shall have been encreased during such time; and no Person holding any Office under the United States, shall be a Member of either House during his Continuance in Office.

Section 7

1: All Bills for raising Revenue shall originate in the House of Representatives; but the Senate may propose or concur with Amendments as on other Bills.

2: Every Bill which shall have passed the House of Representatives and the Senate, shall, before it become a Law, be presented to the President of the United States; If he approve he shall sign it, but if not he shall return it, with his Objections to that House in which it shall have originated, who shall enter the Objections at large on their Journal, and proceed to reconsider it. If after such Reconsideration two thirds of that House shall agree to pass the Bill, it shall be sent, together with the Objections, to the other House, by which it shall likewise be reconsidered, and if approved by two thirds of that House, it shall become a Law. But in all such Cases the Votes of both Houses shall be determined by yeas and Nays, and the Names of the Persons voting for and against the Bill shall be entered on the Journal of each House respectively. If any Bill shall not be returned by the President within ten Days (Sundays excepted) after it shall have been presented to him, the Same shall be a Law, in like Manner as if he had signed it, unless the Congress by their Adjournment prevent its Return, in which Case it shall not be a Law.

3: Every Order, Resolution, or Vote to which the Concurrence of the Senate and House of Representatives may be necessary (except on a question of Adjournment) shall be presented to the President of the United States; and before the Same shall take Effect, shall be approved by him, or being disapproved by him, shall be repassed by two thirds of the Senate and House of Representatives, according to the Rules and Limitations prescribed in the Case of a Bill.

---

[5] Article 1 Section 6 Clause 1 has been affected by Amendment XXVII.

Section 8

1: The Congress shall have Power To lay and collect Taxes, Duties, Imposts and Excises, to pay the Debts and provide for the common Defence and general Welfare of the United States; but all Duties, Imposts and Excises shall be uniform throughout the United States;

2: To borrow Money on the credit of the United States;

3: To regulate Commerce with foreign Nations, and among the several States, and with the Indian Tribes;

4: To establish an uniform Rule of Naturalization, and uniform Laws on the subject of Bankruptcies throughout the United States;

5: To coin Money, regulate the Value thereof, and of foreign Coin, and fix the Standard of Weights and Measures;

6: To provide for the Punishment of counterfeiting the Securities and current Coin of the United States;

7: To establish Post Offices and post Roads;

8: To promote the Progress of Science and useful Arts, by securing for limited Times to Authors and Inventors the exclusive Right to their respective Writings and Discoveries;

9: To constitute Tribunals inferior to the supreme Court;

10: To define and punish Piracies and Felonies committed on the high Seas, and Offences against the Law of Nations;

11: To declare War, grant Letters of Marque and Reprisal, and make Rules concerning Captures on Land and Water;

12: To raise and support Armies, but no Appropriation of Money to that Use shall be for a longer Term than two Years;

13: To provide and maintain a Navy;

14: To make Rules for the Government and Regulation of the land and naval Forces;

15: To provide for calling forth the Militia to execute the Laws of the Union, suppress Insurrections and repel Invasions;

16: To provide for organizing, arming, and disciplining, the Militia, and for governing such Part of them as may be employed in the Service of the United States, reserving to the States respectively, the Appointment of the Officers, and the Authority of training the Militia according to the discipline prescribed by Congress;

17: To exercise exclusive Legislation in all Cases whatsoever, over such District (not exceeding ten Miles square) as may, by Cession of particular States, and the Acceptance of Congress, become the Seat of the Government of the United States, and to exercise like Authority over all Places purchased by the Consent of the Legislature of the State in which the Same shall be, for the Erection of Forts, Magazines, Arsenals, dock-Yards, and other needful Buildings;—And

18: To make all Laws which shall be necessary and proper for carrying into Execution the foregoing Powers, and all other Powers vested by this Constitution in the Government of the United States, or in any Department or Officer thereof.

Section 9

1: The Migration or Importation of such Persons as any of the States now existing shall think proper to admit, shall not be prohibited by the Congress prior to the Year one thousand eight hundred and eight, but a Tax or duty may be imposed on such Importation, not exceeding ten dollars for each Person.

2: The Privilege of the Writ of Habeas Corpus shall not be suspended, unless when in Cases of Rebellion or Invasion the public Safety may require it.

3: No Bill of Attainder or ex post facto Law shall be passed.

4: *No Capitation, or other direct, Tax shall be laid, unless in Proportion to the Census or Enumeration herein before directed to be taken.*[6]

5: No Tax or Duty shall be laid on Articles exported from any State.

6: No Preference shall be given by any Regulation of Commerce or Revenue to the Ports of one State over those of another: nor shall Vessels bound to, or from, one State, be obliged to enter, clear, or pay Duties in another.

7: No Money shall be drawn from the Treasury, but in Consequence of Appropriations made by Law; and a regular Statement and Account of the Receipts and Expenditures of all public Money shall be published from time to time.

8: No Title of Nobility shall be granted by the United States: And no Person holding any Office of Profit or Trust under them, shall, without the Consent of the Congress, accept of any present, Emolument, Office, or Title, of any kind whatever, from any King, Prince, or foreign State.

Section 10

1: No State shall enter into any Treaty, Alliance, or Confederation; grant Letters of Marque and Reprisal; coin Money; emit Bills of Credit; make any Thing but gold and silver Coin a Tender in Payment of Debts; pass any Bill of Attainder, ex post facto Law, or Law impairing the Obligation of Contracts, or grant any Title of Nobility.

2: No State shall, without the Consent of the Congress, lay any Imposts or Duties on Imports or Exports, except what may be absolutely necessary for executing it's inspection Laws: and the net Produce of all Duties and Imposts, laid by any State on Imports or Exports, shall be for the Use of the Treasury of the United States; and all such Laws shall be subject to the Revision and Controul of the Congress.

3: No State shall, without the Consent of Congress, lay any Duty of Tonnage, keep Troops, or Ships of War in time of Peace, enter into any Agreement or Compact with another State, or with a foreign Power, or engage in War, unless actually invaded, or in such imminent Danger as will not admit of delay.

---

[6] Article 1 Section 9 Clause 4 has been affected by Amendment XVI.

Article II [Executive Power: The President]

Section 1

1: The executive Power shall be vested in a President of the United States of America. He shall hold his Office during the Term of four Years, and, together with the Vice President, chosen for the same Term, be elected, as follows

2: Each State shall appoint, in such Manner as the Legislature thereof may direct, a Number of Electors, equal to the whole Number of Senators and Representatives to which the State may be entitled in the Congress: but no Senator or Representative, or Person holding an Office of Trust or Profit under the United States, shall be appointed an Elector.

3: *The Electors shall meet in their respective States, and vote by Ballot for two Persons, of whom one at least shall not be an Inhabitant of the same State with themselves. And they shall make a List of all the Persons voted for, and of the Number of Votes for each; which List they shall sign and certify, and transmit sealed to the Seat of the Government of the United States, directed to the President of the Senate. The President of the Senate shall, in the Presence of the Senate and House of Representatives, open all the Certificates, and the Votes shall then be counted. The Person having the greatest Number of Votes shall be the President, if such Number be a Majority of the whole Number of Electors appointed; and if there be more than one who have such Majority, and have an equal Number of Votes, then the House of Representatives shall immediately chuse by Ballot one of them for President; and if no Person have a Majority, then from the five highest on the List the said House shall in like Manner chuse the President. But in chusing the President, the Votes shall be taken by States, the Representation from each State having one Vote; A quorum for this Purpose shall consist of a Member or Members from two thirds of the States, and a Majority of all the States shall be necessary to a Choice. In every Case, after the Choice of the President, the Person having the greatest Number of Votes of the Electors shall be the Vice President. But if there should remain two or more who have equal Votes, the Senate shall chuse from them by Ballot the Vice President.*[7]

4: The Congress may determine the Time of chusing the Electors, and the Day on which they shall give their Votes; which Day shall be the same throughout the United States.

5: No Person except a natural born Citizen, or a Citizen of the United States, at the time of the Adoption of this Constitution, shall be eligible to the Office of President; neither shall any Person be eligible to that Office who shall not have attained to the Age of thirty five Years, and been fourteen Years a Resident within the United States.

6: *In Case of the Removal of the President from Office, or of his Death, Resignation, or Inability to discharge the Powers and Duties of the said Office,* the Same shall devolve on the Vice President, and the Congress may by Law provide for the Case of Removal, Death, Resignation or Inability, both of the President and Vice President, declaring what Officer shall then act as President, and such Officer shall act accordingly, until the Disability be removed, or a President shall be elected.[8]

7: The President shall, at stated Times, receive for his Services, a Compensation, which shall neither be encreased nor diminished during the Period for which he shall have been elected, and he shall not receive within that Period any other Emolument from the United States, or any of them.

---

[7] Article 2 Section 1 Clause 3 has been superseded by Amendment XII.
[8] Article 2 Section 1 Clause 6 has been affected by Amendment XX and Amendment XXV.

8: Before he enter on the Execution of his Office, he shall take the following Oath or Affirmation:—"I do solemnly swear (or affirm) that I will faithfully execute the Office of President of the United States, and will to the best of my Ability, preserve, protect and defend the Constitution of the United States."

Section 2

1: The President shall be Commander in Chief of the Army and Navy of the United States, and of the Militia of the several States, when called into the actual Service of the United States; he may require the Opinion, in writing, of the principal Officer in each of the executive Departments, upon any Subject relating to the Duties of their respective Offices, and he shall have Power to grant Reprieves and Pardons for Offences against the United States, except in Cases of Impeachment.

2: He shall have Power, by and with the Advice and Consent of the Senate, to make Treaties, provided two thirds of the Senators present concur; and he shall nominate, and by and with the Advice and Consent of the Senate, shall appoint Ambassadors, other public Ministers and Consuls, Judges of the supreme Court, and all other Officers of the United States, whose Appointments are not herein otherwise provided for, and which shall be established by Law: but the Congress may by Law vest the Appointment of such inferior Officers, as they think proper, in the President alone, in the Courts of Law, or in the Heads of Departments.

3: The President shall have Power to fill up all Vacancies that may happen during the Recess of the Senate, by granting Commissions which shall expire at the End of their next Session.

Section 3

He shall from time to time give to the Congress Information of the State of the Union, and recommend to their Consideration such Measures as he shall judge necessary and expedient; he may, on extraordinary Occasions, convene both Houses, or either of them, and in Case of Disagreement between them, with Respect to the Time of Adjournment, he may adjourn them to such Time as he shall think proper; he shall receive Ambassadors and other public Ministers; he shall take Care that the Laws be faithfully executed, and shall Commission all the Officers of the United States.

Section 4

The President, Vice President and all civil Officers of the United States, shall be removed from Office on Impeachment for, and Conviction of, Treason, Bribery, or other high Crimes and Misdemeanors.

Article III [Judicial Power: The Federal Courts]

Section 1

The judicial Power of the United States, shall be vested in one supreme Court, and in such inferior Courts as the Congress may from time to time ordain and establish. The Judges, both of the supreme and inferior Courts, shall hold their Offices during good Behaviour, and shall, at stated Times, receive for their Services, a Compensation, which shall not be diminished during their Continuance in Office.

Section 2

1: The judicial Power shall extend to all Cases, in Law and Equity, arising under this Constitution, the Laws of the United States, and Treaties made, or which shall be made, under their Authority;—to all Cases affecting Ambassadors, other public Ministers and Consuls;—to all Cases of admiralty and maritime Jurisdiction;—to Controversies to which the United States shall be a Party;—to Controversies between two or more States;—*between a State and Citizens of another State;*[9] —between Citizens of different States, —between Citizens of the same State claiming Lands under Grants of different States, and between a State, or the Citizens thereof, and foreign States, Citizens or Subjects.

2: In all Cases affecting Ambassadors, other public Ministers and Consuls, and those in which a State shall be Party, the supreme Court shall have original Jurisdiction. In all the other Cases before mentioned, the supreme Court shall have appellate Jurisdiction, both as to Law and Fact, with such Exceptions, and under such Regulations as the Congress shall make.

3: The Trial of all Crimes, except in Cases of Impeachment, shall be by Jury; and such Trial shall be held in the State where the said Crimes shall have been committed; but when not committed within any State, the Trial shall be at such Place or Places as the Congress may by Law have directed.

Section 3

1: Treason against the United States, shall consist only in levying War against them, or in adhering to their Enemies, giving them Aid and Comfort. No Person shall be convicted of Treason unless on the Testimony of two Witnesses to the same overt Act, or on Confession in open Court.

2: The Congress shall have Power to declare the Punishment of Treason, but no Attainder of Treason shall work Corruption of Blood, or Forfeiture except during the Life of the Person attainted.

Article IV [Relations between the States]

Section 1

Full Faith and Credit shall be given in each State to the public Acts, Records, and judicial Proceedings of every other State. And the Congress may by general Laws prescribe the Manner in which such Acts, Records and Proceedings shall be proved, and the Effect thereof.

Section 2

1: The Citizens of each State shall be entitled to all Privileges and Immunities of Citizens in the several States.

2: A Person charged in any State with Treason, Felony, or other Crime, who shall flee from Justice, and be found in another State, shall on Demand of the executive Authority of the State from which he fled, be delivered up, to be removed to the State having Jurisdiction of the Crime.

---

[9] Article 3 Section 2 Clause 1 has been affected by Amendment XI.

3: No Person held to Service or Labour in one State, under the Laws thereof, escaping into another, shall, in Consequence of any Law or Regulation therein, be discharged from such Service or Labour, but shall be delivered up on Claim of the Party to whom such Service or Labour may be due.[10]

Section 3

1: New States may be admitted by the Congress into this Union; but no new State shall be formed or erected within the Jurisdiction of any other State; nor any State be formed by the Junction of two or more States, or Parts of States, without the Consent of the Legislatures of the States concerned as well as of the Congress.

2: The Congress shall have Power to dispose of and make all needful Rules and Regulations respecting the Territory or other Property belonging to the United States; and nothing in this Constitution shall be so construed as to Prejudice any Claims of the United States, or of any particular State.

Section 4

The United States shall guarantee to every State in this Union a Republican Form of Government, and shall protect each of them against Invasion; and on Application of the Legislature, or of the Executive (when the Legislature cannot be convened) against domestic Violence.

Article V [Amending the Constitution]

The Congress, whenever two thirds of both Houses shall deem it necessary, shall propose Amendments to this Constitution, or, on the Application of the Legislatures of two thirds of the several States, shall call a Convention for proposing Amendments, which, in either Case, shall be valid to all Intents and Purposes, as Part of this Constitution, when ratified by the Legislatures of three fourths of the several States, or by Conventions in three fourths thereof, as the one or the other Mode of Ratification may be proposed by the Congress; Provided that no Amendment which may be made prior to the Year One thousand eight hundred and eight shall in any Manner affect the first and fourth Clauses in the Ninth Section of the first Article; and that no State, without its Consent, shall be deprived of its equal Suffrage in the Senate.

Article VI [Prior debts, Supremacy Clause, No Religious Test for Office]

1: All Debts contracted and Engagements entered into, before the Adoption of this Constitution, shall be as valid against the United States under this Constitution, as under the Confederation.

2: This Constitution, and the Laws of the United States which shall be made in Pursuance thereof; and all Treaties made, or which shall be made, under the Authority of the United States, shall be the supreme Law of the Land; and the Judges in every State shall be bound thereby, any Thing in the Constitution or Laws of any State to the Contrary notwithstanding.

3: The Senators and Representatives before mentioned, and the Members of the several State Legislatures, and all executive and judicial Officers, both of the United States and of the several States, shall be bound by Oath or Affirmation, to support this Constitution; but no religious Test shall ever be required as a Qualification to any Office or public Trust under the United States.

---

[10] Article 4 Section 2 Clause 3 has been affected by Amendment XIII Section 1.

Article VII [Ratification Procedure]

The Ratification of the Conventions of nine States, shall be sufficient for the Establishment of this Constitution between the States so ratifying the Same.

The Word "the", being interlined between the seventh and eight Lines of the first Page, The Word "Thirty" being partly written on an Erazure in the fifteenth Line of the first Page. The Words "is tried" being interlined between the thirty second and thirty third Lines of the first Page and the Word "the" being interlined between the forty third and forty fourth Lines of the second Page.

Done in Convention by the Unanimous Consent of the States present the Seventeenth Day of September in the Year of our Lord one thousand seven hundred and Eighty seven and of the Independence of the United States of America the Twelfth **In witness** whereof We have hereunto subscribed our Names,

---

Go: Washington -Presidt. and deputy from Virginia

Delaware
Geo: Read
Gunning Bedford jun
John Dickinson
Richard Bassett
Jaco: Broom

Maryland
James McHenry
Dan of St Thos. Jenifer
Danl Carroll.

Virginia
John Blair—
James Madison Jr.

North Carolina
Wm Blount
Richd. Dobbs Spaight.
Hu Williamson

South Carolina
J. Rutledge
Charles Cotesworth Pinckney
Charles Pinckney
Pierce Butler.

Georgia
William Few
Abr Baldwin

New Hampshire
John Langdon
Nicholas Gilman

Massachusetts
Nathaniel Gorham
Rufus King

Connecticut
Wm. Saml. Johnson
Roger Sherman

New York
Alexander Hamilton

New Jersey
Wil. Livingston
David Brearley.
Wm. Paterson.
Jona: Dayton

Pennsylvania
B Franklin
Thomas Mifflin
Robt Morris
Geo. Clymer
Thos. FitzSimons
Jared Ingersoll
James Wilson.
Gouv Morris

Amendments to the United State Constitution

[Preamble to the Bill of Rights, Amendments I-X]

> Congress of the United States, begun and held at the City of New-York, on Wednesday the fourth of March, one thousand seven hundred and eighty nine.
> THE Conventions of a number of the States, having at the time of their adopting the Constitution, expressed a desire, in order to prevent misconstruction or abuse of its powers, that further declaratory and restrictive clauses should be added: And as extending the ground of public confidence in the Government, will best ensure the beneficent ends of its institution.

Amendment I [Freedom of Religion, Expression, and the Press]

Congress shall make no law respecting an establishment of religion, or prohibiting the free exercise thereof; or abridging the freedom of speech, or of the press; or the right of the people peaceably to assemble, and to petition the Government for a redress of grievances.

Amendment II [Right to bear arms]

A well regulated Militia, being necessary to the security of a free State, the right of the people to keep and bear Arms, shall not be infringed.

Amendment III [Quartering soldiers]

No Soldier shall, in time of peace be quartered in any house, without the consent of the Owner, nor in time of war, but in a manner to be prescribed by law.

Amendment IV [Unreasonable searches and seizures]

The right of the people to be secure in their persons, houses, papers, and effects, against unreasonable searches and seizures, shall not be violated, and no Warrants shall issue, but upon probable cause, supported by Oath or affirmation, and particularly describing the place to be searched, and the persons or things to be seized.

Amendment V [Rights of the accused]

No person shall be held to answer for a capital, or otherwise infamous crime, unless on a presentment or indictment of a Grand Jury, except in cases arising in the land or naval forces, or in the Militia, when in actual service in time of War or public danger; nor shall any person be subject for the same offence to be twice put in jeopardy of life or limb; nor shall be compelled in any criminal case to be a witness against himself, nor be deprived of life, liberty, or property, without due process of law; nor shall private property be taken for public use, without just compensation.

Amendment VI [Rights at trial]

In all criminal prosecutions, the accused shall enjoy the right to a speedy and public trial, by an impartial jury of the State and district wherein the crime shall have been committed, which district shall have been previously ascertained by law, and to be informed of the nature and cause of the accusation; to be confronted with the witnesses against him; to have compulsory process for obtaining witnesses in his favor, and to have the Assistance of Counsel for his defence.

Amendment VII [Civil trials]

In Suits at common law, where the value in controversy shall exceed twenty dollars, the right of trial by jury shall be preserved, and no fact tried by a jury, shall be otherwise re-examined in any Court of the United States, than according to the rules of the common law.

Amendment VIII [Excessive punishment]

Excessive bail shall not be required, nor excessive fines imposed, nor cruel and unusual punishments inflicted.

Amendment IX [Unenumerated Rights]

The enumeration in the Constitution, of certain rights, shall not be construed to deny or disparage others retained by the people.

Amendment X [Powers reserved to the states and the people]

The powers not delegated to the United States by the Constitution, nor prohibited by it to the States, are reserved to the States respectively, or to the people.

Amendment XI [Lawsuits against states and across state lines]

Passed by Congress March 4, 1794. Ratified February 7, 1795.

Note: Article III, section 2, of the Constitution was modified by Amendment XI.

The Judicial power of the United States shall not be construed to extend to any suit in law or equity, commenced or prosecuted against one of the United States by Citizens of another State, or by Citizens or Subjects of any Foreign State.

Amendment XII [Modifying the Electoral College]

Passed by Congress December 9, 1803. Ratified June 15, 1804.

Note: Article II, section 1, Clause 3 of the Constitution was superseded by Amendment XII.

The Electors shall meet in their respective states and vote by ballot for President and Vice-President, one of whom, at least, shall not be an inhabitant of the same state with themselves; they shall name in their ballots the person voted for as President, and in distinct ballots the person voted for as Vice-President, and they shall make distinct lists of all persons voted for as President, and of all persons voted for as Vice-President, and of the number of votes for each, which lists they shall sign and certify, and transmit sealed to the seat of the government of the United States, directed to the President of the Senate; -- the President of the Senate shall, in the presence of the Senate and House of Representatives, open all the certificates and the votes shall then be counted; -- The person having the greatest number of votes for President, shall be the President, if such number be a majority of the whole number of Electors appointed; and if no person have such majority, then from the persons having the highest numbers not exceeding three on the list of those voted for as President, the House of Representatives shall choose immediately, by ballot, the President. But in choosing the President, the votes shall be taken by states, the representation from each state having one vote; a quorum for this purpose shall consist of a member or members from two-thirds of the states, and a majority of all the states shall be necessary to a choice. *And if the House of Representatives shall not choose a President whenever the right of choice shall devolve upon them, before the fourth day of March next following, then the Vice-President shall act as President, as in case of the death or other constitutional disability of the President.*[11] The person having the greatest number of votes as Vice-President, shall be the Vice-President, if such number be a majority of the whole number of Electors appointed, and if no person have a majority, then from the two highest numbers on the list, the Senate shall choose the Vice-President; a quorum for the purpose shall consist of two-thirds of the whole number of Senators, and a majority of the whole number shall be necessary to a choice. But no person constitutionally ineligible to the office of President shall be

---

[11] This sentence of Amendment XII has been superseded by Amendment XX Section 3.

eligible to that of Vice-President of the United States. *Superseded by section 3 of the 20th amendment.

Amendment XIII [Prohibit Slavery and Involuntary Servitude]

Passed by Congress January 31, 1865. Ratified December 6, 1865.

Note: Article IV, section 2, clause 3 of the Constitution was superseded by Amendment XIII.

Section 1.

Neither slavery nor involuntary servitude, except as a punishment for crime whereof the party shall have been duly convicted, shall exist within the United States, or any place subject to their jurisdiction.

Section 2.

Congress shall have power to enforce this article by appropriate legislation.

Amendment XIV [Citizenship, State due process and equal protection]

Passed by Congress June 13, 1866. Ratified July 9, 1868.

Note: Article I, section 2, clause 3 of the Constitution was modified by section 2 of Amendment XIV.

Section 1.

All persons born or naturalized in the United States, and subject to the jurisdiction thereof, are citizens of the United States and of the State wherein they reside. No State shall make or enforce any law which shall abridge the privileges or immunities of citizens of the United States; nor shall any State deprive any person of life, liberty, or property, without due process of law; nor deny to any person within its jurisdiction the equal protection of the laws.

Section 2.

Representatives shall be apportioned among the several States according to their respective numbers, counting the whole number of persons in each State, excluding Indians not taxed. But when the right to vote at any election for the choice of electors for President and Vice-President of the United States, Representatives in Congress, the Executive and Judicial officers of a State, or the members of the Legislature thereof, is denied to any of the *male inhabitants* of such State, being *twenty-one years of age*, and citizens of the United States, or in any way abridged, except for participation in rebellion, or other crime, the basis of representation therein shall be reduced in the proportion which the number of such *male citizens* shall bear to the whole number *of male citizens twenty-one years of age* in such State.[12]

Section 3.

No person shall be a Senator or Representative in Congress, or elector of President and Vice-President, or hold any office, civil or military, under the United States, or under any State, who, having previously taken an oath, as a member of Congress, or as an officer of the United States, or as a member of any State legislature, or as an executive or judicial officer of any State, to support the Constitution of the United States, shall have engaged in insurrection or rebellion against the same, or

---

[12] Article XIV Section 2 is modified by Amendment XIX Section 1 (right to vote cannot be denied on the basis of sex) and Amendment XXVI Section 1 (lowering the voting age to 18 years of age).

given aid or comfort to the enemies thereof. But Congress may by a vote of two-thirds of each House, remove such disability.

Section 4.

The validity of the public debt of the United States, authorized by law, including debts incurred for payment of pensions and bounties for services in suppressing insurrection or rebellion, shall not be questioned. But neither the United States nor any State shall assume or pay any debt or obligation incurred in aid of insurrection or rebellion against the United States, or any claim for the loss or emancipation of any slave; but all such debts, obligations and claims shall be held illegal and void.

Section 5.

The Congress shall have the power to enforce, by appropriate legislation, the provisions of this article.

Amendment XV [Right to vote guaranteed for people of color and previous slaves]

Passed by Congress February 26, 1869. Ratified February 3, 1870.

Section 1.

The right of citizens of the United States to vote shall not be denied or abridged by the United States or by any State on account of race, color, or previous condition of servitude--

Section 2.

The Congress shall have the power to enforce this article by appropriate legislation.

Amendment XVI [Income tax]

Passed by Congress July 2, 1909. Ratified February 3, 1913.

Note: Article I, section 9, clause 4 of the Constitution was modified by Amendment XVI.

The Congress shall have power to lay and collect taxes on incomes, from whatever source derived, without apportionment among the several States, and without regard to any census or enumeration.

Amendment XVII [Popular Election of Senators]

Passed by Congress May 13, 1912. Ratified April 8, 1913.

Note: Article I, section 3, clause 2 of the Constitution was modified by Amendment XVII.

The Senate of the United States shall be composed of two Senators from each State, elected by the people thereof, for six years; and each Senator shall have one vote. The electors in each State shall have the qualifications requisite for electors of the most numerous branch of the State legislatures.

When vacancies happen in the representation of any State in the Senate, the executive authority of such State shall issue writs of election to fill such vacancies: Provided, that the legislature of any State may empower the executive thereof to make temporary appointments until the people fill the vacancies by election as the legislature may direct.

This amendment shall not be so construed as to affect the election or term of any Senator chosen before it becomes valid as part of the Constitution.

Amendment XVIII [13] [Prohibition]

Passed by Congress December 18, 1917. Ratified January 16, 1919. Repealed by Amendment XXI.

Section 1.

After one year from the ratification of this article the manufacture, sale, or transportation of intoxicating liquors within, the importation thereof into, or the exportation thereof from the United States and all territory subject to the jurisdiction thereof for beverage purposes is hereby prohibited.

Section 2.

The Congress and the several States shall have concurrent power to enforce this article by appropriate legislation.

Section 3.

This article shall be inoperative unless it shall have been ratified as an amendment to the Constitution by the legislatures of the several States, as provided in the Constitution, within seven years from the date of the submission hereof to the States by the Congress.

Amendment XIX [Right to vote guaranteed to women]

Passed by Congress June 4, 1919. Ratified August 18, 1920.

Note: Amendment XIV, Section 2 is modified by Amendment XIX.

The right of citizens of the United States to vote shall not be denied or abridged by the United States or by any State on account of sex.

Congress shall have power to enforce this article by appropriate legislation.

Amendment XX [Change dates of office, Presidential vacancy]

Passed by Congress March 2, 1932. Ratified January 23, 1933.

Note: Article I, section 4, of the Constitution was modified by section 2 of this amendment. In addition, a portion of Amendment XII was superseded by section 3

Section 1.

The terms of the President and the Vice President shall end at noon on the 20th day of January, and the terms of Senators and Representatives at noon on the 3d day of January, of the years in which such terms would have ended if this article had not been ratified; and the terms of their successors shall then begin.

Section 2.

The Congress shall assemble at least once in every year, and such meeting shall begin at noon on the 3d day of January, unless they shall by law appoint a different day.

Section 3.

If, at the time fixed for the beginning of the term of the President, the President elect shall have died, the Vice President elect shall become President. If a President shall not have been chosen before the time fixed for the beginning of his term, or if the President elect shall have failed to qualify, then the

---

[13] Amendment XVIII repealed by Amendment XXI Section 1.

Vice President elect shall act as President until a President shall have qualified; and the Congress may by law provide for the case wherein neither a President elect nor a Vice President elect shall have qualified, declaring who shall then act as President, or the manner in which one who is to act shall be selected, and such person shall act accordingly until a President or Vice President shall have qualified.

Section 4.

The Congress may by law provide for the case of the death of any of the persons from whom the House of Representatives may choose a President whenever the right of choice shall have devolved upon them, and for the case of the death of any of the persons from whom the Senate may choose a Vice President whenever the right of choice shall have devolved upon them.

Section 5.

Sections 1 and 2 shall take effect on the 15th day of October following the ratification of this article.

Section 6.

This article shall be inoperative unless it shall have been ratified as an amendment to the Constitution by the legislatures of three-fourths of the several States within seven years from the date of its submission.

Amendment XXI [Repeal Prohibition Amendment XVIII]

Passed by Congress February 20, 1933. Ratified December 5, 1933.

Section 1.

The eighteenth article of amendment to the Constitution of the United States is hereby repealed.

Section 2.

The transportation or importation into any State, Territory, or possession of the United States for delivery or use therein of intoxicating liquors, in violation of the laws thereof, is hereby prohibited.

Section 3.

This article shall be inoperative unless it shall have been ratified as an amendment to the Constitution by conventions in the several States, as provided in the Constitution, within seven years from the date of the submission hereof to the States by the Congress.

Amendment XXII [Presidential term limits]

Passed by Congress March 21, 1947. Ratified February 27, 1951.

Section 1.

No person shall be elected to the office of the President more than twice, and no person who has held the office of President, or acted as President, for more than two years of a term to which some other person was elected President shall be elected to the office of the President more than once. But this Article shall not apply to any person holding the office of President when this Article was proposed by the Congress, and shall not prevent any person who may be holding the office of President, or acting as President, during the term within which this Article becomes operative from holding the office of President or acting as President during the remainder of such term.

Section 2.

This article shall be inoperative unless it shall have been ratified as an amendment to the Constitution by the legislatures of three-fourths of the several States within seven years from the date of its submission to the States by the Congress.

Amendment XXIII [Washington, DC presidential Electors]

Passed by Congress June 16, 1960. Ratified March 29, 1961.

Section 1.

The District constituting the seat of Government of the United States shall appoint in such manner as the Congress may direct:

A number of electors of President and Vice President equal to the whole number of Senators and Representatives in Congress to which the District would be entitled if it were a State, but in no event more than the least populous State; they shall be in addition to those appointed by the States, but they shall be considered, for the purposes of the election of President and Vice President, to be electors appointed by a State; and they shall meet in the District and perform such duties as provided by the twelfth article of amendment.

Section 2.

The Congress shall have power to enforce this article by appropriate legislation.

Amendment XXIV [Prohibit poll taxes]

Passed by Congress August 27, 1962. Ratified January 23, 1964.

Section 1.

The right of citizens of the United States to vote in any primary or other election for President or Vice President, for electors for President or Vice President, or for Senator or Representative in Congress, shall not be denied or abridged by the United States or any State by reason of failure to pay any poll tax or other tax.

Section 2.

The Congress shall have power to enforce this article by appropriate legislation.

Amendment XXV [Presidential succession or disability]

Passed by Congress July 6, 1965. Ratified February 10, 1967.

Note: Article II, section 1, of the Constitution was affected by Amendment XXV.

Section 1.

In case of the removal of the President from office or of his death or resignation, the Vice President shall become President.

Section 2.

Whenever there is a vacancy in the office of the Vice President, the President shall nominate a Vice President who shall take office upon confirmation by a majority vote of both Houses of Congress.

Section 3.

Whenever the President transmits to the President pro tempore of the Senate and the Speaker of the House of Representatives his written declaration that he is unable to discharge the powers and duties of his office, and until he transmits to them a written declaration to the contrary, such powers and duties shall be discharged by the Vice President as Acting President.

Section 4.

Whenever the Vice President and a majority of either the principal officers of the executive departments or of such other body as Congress may by law provide, transmit to the President pro tempore of the Senate and the Speaker of the House of Representatives their written declaration that the President is unable to discharge the powers and duties of his office, the Vice President shall immediately assume the powers and duties of the office as Acting President.

Thereafter, when the President transmits to the President pro tempore of the Senate and the Speaker of the House of Representatives his written declaration that no inability exists, he shall resume the powers and duties of his office unless the Vice President and a majority of either the principal officers of the executive department or of such other body as Congress may by law provide, transmit within four days to the President pro tempore of the Senate and the Speaker of the House of Representatives their written declaration that the President is unable to discharge the powers and duties of his office. Thereupon Congress shall decide the issue, assembling within forty-eight hours for that purpose if not in session. If the Congress, within twenty-one days after receipt of the latter written declaration, or, if Congress is not in session, within twenty-one days after Congress is required to assemble, determines by two-thirds vote of both Houses that the President is unable to discharge the powers and duties of his office, the Vice President shall continue to discharge the same as Acting President; otherwise, the President shall resume the powers and duties of his office.

Amendment XXVI [Lower voting age to 18 years]

Passed by Congress March 23, 1971. Ratified July 1, 1971.

Note: Amendment XIV, section 2, of the Constitution was modified by Amendment XXVI, section 1.

Section 1.

The right of citizens of the United States, who are eighteen years of age or older, to vote shall not be denied or abridged by the United States or by any State on account of age.

Section 2.

The Congress shall have power to enforce this article by appropriate legislation.

Amendment XXVII [Require election before a congressional pay increase]

Originally proposed Sept. 25, 1789. Ratified May 7, 1992.

No law, varying the compensation for the services of the Senators and Representatives, shall take effect, until an election of Representatives shall have intervened.

Text and annotations adapted from https://constitutionus.com/ and "The Constitution of the United States: A Transcription." National Archives, 4 Nov. 2015, www.archives.gov/founding-docs/constitution-transcript.

Chapter 1. Why Government? Why Politics?

Studying the Chapter Content

- ❏ Read the introductory paragraphs at the beginning of the chapter.
- ❏ Read the "Summary" paragraphs at the end of the chapter.
- ❏ Scan the chapter, noting the major headings and subheadings, and bolded vocabulary terms
- ❏ Take note of tables and figures in the chapter.
- ❏ Review the study questions in this guide for the chapter, and note how they correspond to the major sections of the chapter.
- ❏ Based on your survey of the major headings and subheadings of the chapter, generate a set of your own questions about the chapter.
- ❏ Read the chapter carefully in light of the study guide questions and the questions you have developed. Consider dividing your reading and study time into 2-3 subsections at a time.
- ❏ Outline the chapter, noting key concepts and the authors' conclusions.
- ❏ Review the study guide questions and your own study questions, attempting to address those questions in your own words.
- ❏ Make flashcards for the vocabulary terms and key concepts, and study them regularly.
- ❏ Review your notes as needed to prepare for the first assessment.
- ❏ Review your notes and the text as needed to prepare for subsequent assessments.

Chapter 1 Study Questions

1. Why is government necessary? What are the three sectors of organized life in political communities? How do they organize life? What is the *power problem*? What does *justice* mean in our constitutional system? What are the different ways of conceiving what justice is?
2. What is the social contract theory of government and why is it important? Who are the main people associated with social contract theory? Who and what were they key influences on America's Founders?
3. What are the main roles of modern governments? How do these differ from anarchism? How do *market failures* relate to politics, government, and justifying government action? What are the major types of relevant market failures and how has government responded?
4. How do conceptions of politics differ? What is political science?
5. What are the core political values of American society? What are the differences between negative and positive conceptions of liberty? What are the differences between power, authority, and legitimacy?
6. What does it mean to be a citizen? Why is citizenship important?
7. What are the good and bad versions of the different forms of government? What form of government does the United States have? How is this different from direct democracy?

Vocabulary Terms & Key Concepts

Anarchism
Authority
Citizenship

Market Failures
Politics
Power

- Civil Society
- Direct Democracy
- Distributive justice
- Equality
- Government
- Justice
- Legitimacy
- Liberty
- The Power Problem
- Public Good
- Representative Democracy
- Republic
- Retributive justice
- Restorative justice
- Social Contract
- Social order

Chapter 2. The U.S. System of Constitutional Government

Studying the Chapter Content

- ☐ Read the *Declaration of Independence* and scan/survey the US Constitution.
- ☐ Read the introductory paragraphs at the beginning of the chapter.
- ☐ Read the "Summary" paragraphs at the end of the chapter.
- ☐ Scan the chapter, noting the major headings and subheadings, and bolded vocabulary terms
- ☐ Take note of tables and figures in the chapter.
- ☐ Review the study questions in this guide for the chapter, and note how they correspond to the major sections of the chapter.
- ☐ Based on your survey of the major headings and subheadings of the chapter, generate a set of your own questions about the chapter.
- ☐ Read the chapter carefully in light of the study guide questions and the questions you have developed. Consider dividing your reading and study time into 2-3 subsections at a time.
- ☐ Outline the chapter, noting key concepts and the authors' conclusions.
- ☐ Review the study guide questions and your own study questions, attempting to address those questions in your own words.
- ☐ Make flashcards for the vocabulary terms and key concepts, and study them regularly.
- ☐ Review your notes as needed to prepare for the first assessment.
- ☐ Review your notes and the text as needed to prepare for subsequent assessments.

Chapter 2 Study Questions

1. Why do nations have constitutions? What roles does a constitution play?
2. What is the "Rule of Law" and why is it important? How do the constitution and Rule of Law interact for the United States?
3. What are the components of the *American Creed*? What does it mean to say the US is a *constitutional democracy*? What were the major eras of US constitutional development?
4. What were the important political conflicts during the Founding Era? What factors fostered the spirit of independence in the American colonies? What factors led to the drafting of the Declaration of Independence?
5. What was the role of the Articles of Confederation? What were the problems with the Articles? How were these problems addressed in the second US Constitution? What are the main things the US Constitution does? What are the roles of federalism, separation of powers, and the republican form of government? How does the constitution guarantee individual rights and freedoms? What was the role of the Bill of Rights in the ratification debates, and what is its role today? What is the difference between *civil liberties* and *civil rights*?
6. How do Americans today think about the constitution, and how does our constitution interact with the political system generally? In what ways has the American system evolved apart from or in spite of the constitution?

Key terms and concepts

American Creed	Civil Rights	The Federalist Papers
Articles of Confederation	Confederation	Ratification
Bill of Rights	Constitution	Rule of Law
Checks and balances	Constitutional democracy	Separation of powers

Civil Liberties   Federalism   Shays' Rebellion

Key dates

1775: American Revolutionary War begins
1776: Declaration of Independence
1777: Articles of Confederation written
1787: Constitutional Convention

1789: Bill of Rights drafted
1791: Second US Constitution ratified
1808: Importation of slaves prohibited

Chapter 6. Federalism

Studying the Chapter Content

- Read Article I Section 10; Article IV; Article VI Sections 2 and 3; Article VII; and Amendments X, XIV Section 1.
- Read the introductory paragraphs at the beginning of the chapter.
- Read the "Summary" paragraphs at the end of the chapter.
- Scan the chapter, noting the major headings and subheadings, and bolded vocabulary terms
- Take note of tables and figures in the chapter.
- Review the study questions in this guide for the chapter, and note how they correspond to the major sections of the chapter.
- Based on your survey of the major headings and subheadings of the chapter, generate a set of your own questions about the chapter.
- Read the chapter carefully in light of the study guide questions and the questions you have developed. Consider dividing your reading and study time into 2-3 subsections at a time.
- Outline the chapter, noting key concepts and the authors' conclusions.
- Review the study guide questions and your own study questions, attempting to address those questions in your own words.
- Make flashcards for the vocabulary terms and key concepts, and study them regularly.
- Review your notes as needed to prepare for the first assessment.
- Review your notes and the text as needed to prepare for subsequent assessments.

Chapter 6 Study Questions

1. What is federalism? What is the power problem as it relates to federalism? What three purposes does federalism serve? What is the difference between a federal system, unitary system, and a confederal system?
2. How did the Articles of Confederation distribute government power? What was the Second Confederation?
3. How does the constitution distribute powers in federalism?
4. Why did the Federalists believe that a strong federal government was necessary?
5. What have been the two major political effects of federalism?
6. What does the text mean when it says that federalism is dynamic? What were dual federalism and cooperative federalism? How and why has federal (national government) power expanded? Why and in what ways have some opposed this expansion?
7. What is "New" federalism and how was it a response to federal government expansion? How do immigration laws reflect the conflicts inherent in federalism? How have the courts resolved those conflicts?

Key terms and concepts

Confederation	Federalism	Preemption
Cooperative federalism	Intergovernmental relations	States' rights
Cooley Doctrine	Interposition	Unitary system
Dual federalism	New Federalism	

Chapter 6 Court Cases to Know

Arizona v. US (2012)
United States v. Lopez (1995)

Chapter 16. Civil Liberties and Civil Rights

Studying the Chapter Content

- Read the US Constitution Article I Section 9; the Bill of Rights; and Amendments XIII, XIV, XV, XIX, XXIV, and XXVI.
- Read the introductory paragraphs at the beginning of the chapter.
- Read the "Summary" paragraphs at the end of the chapter.
- Scan the chapter, noting the major headings and subheadings, and bolded vocabulary terms
- Take note of tables and figures in the chapter.
- Review the study questions in this guide for the chapter, and note how they correspond to the major sections of the chapter.
- Based on your survey of the major headings and subheadings of the chapter, generate a set of your own questions about the chapter.
- Read the chapter carefully in light of the study guide questions and the questions you have developed. Consider dividing your reading and study time into 2-3 subsections at a time.
- Outline the chapter, noting key concepts and the authors' conclusions.
- Review the study guide questions and your own study questions, attempting to address those questions in your own words.
- Make flashcards for the vocabulary terms and key concepts, and study them regularly.
- Review your notes as needed to prepare for the first assessment.
- Review your notes and the text as needed to prepare for subsequent assessments.

Chapter 16 Study Questions

Note: In the Crime Policy section of chapter 16, I will test on the crime policy and civil liberties sections of the chapter (sections 16.0 through 16.65), but not the criminal justice section (16.7)

1. How does the text define *civil liberties*? How does it define *civil rights*? What are the main differences between civil liberties and civil rights? Why do you think the text calls some people's exercise of freedom of expression as "uncivil liberties"?
2. What liberties are protected by the First Amendment? What is the *Establishment Clause*? What are the two major interpretations of the First Amendment's Establishment Clause? What were the provisions of the *Lemon Test*? What is the *Free Exercise Clause*? What two principles emerged from <u>Reynolds v. US</u> that relate to the free exercise of religion? How has the Supreme Court attempted to define religion? What is *content neutrality*? What are the *reasonableness test* and *strict scrutiny test*? How does the contemporary Supreme Court seem to be approaching free exercise cases?
3. What is meant by *Freedom of Speech*?
4. How did *equality* become an important political and legal value? Does Equality mean treating everyone the same? Why or why not? Explain *Equal Protection of the Laws*. What was the constitutional revolution of 1937, and why was it important? How did racial classifications evolve? What was the *Separate but Equal Doctrine*? How did American schools come to be desegregated? How have the courts distinguished between *de jure* segregation and *de facto* segregation? How have sex- or gender-based differences changed

in their treatment by the law and courts? What was the *gender difference rationale*? What were the major statutes addressing sex/gender discrimination? How are citizens, aliens, and non-residents treated under the law?
5. What are the two basic theories explaining the causes of crime? What are the main differences between those theories? What two models of justice does the text use to explain differences in liberal and conservative thinking about crime? What are the main differences between them? What kinds of questions are raised as social scientists attempt to explain changing rates of incarceration?
6. In general, how do the Second, Fourth, Fifth, and Sixth Amendments protect citizens from the government? What right is protected by the Second Amendment and what are the limitations on that right? What has the Fourth Amendment protection come to mean, and to what extent are there exceptions to that protection? What is the importance of the *Exclusionary Rule*? How does the Fifth Amendment protect citizens? How does the Sixth Amendment protect citizens?

Key terms and concepts

Accommodation
Alienage
Bill of Rights
Civil liberties
Civil rights
Civil Rights Act of 1964
Civil War Amendments
Content neutrality
De facto segregation
De jure segregation
Discrimination
Establishment clause
Exclusionary rule
Free exercise clause
Freedom of religion
Freedom of speech
Freedom of the press
Freedom to assemble
Freedom to petition the government
Gender difference rationale
Human nature theory of crime
Incarceration rates
Lemon test
Liberal order
Paternalistic
Religious Freedom Restoration Act
Republican order
Separate but Equal Doctrine
Social theory of crime
Title IX
Unreasonable search and seizure
Voting Rights Act of 1965
Wall of separation

Chapter 16 Court Cases to Know

Civil Liberties
Reynolds v. U.S. (1879)
Schenck v. United States (1919); discussed on p. 425
Powell v. Alabama (1932)
Mapp v. Ohio (1961)
Miranda v. Arizona (1966)
Katz v. U.S. (1967)
Lemon v. Kurtzman (1971)
Texas v. Johnson (1989); discussed on p. 425
Employment Division of Oregon v. Smith (1990)
District of Columbia v. Heller (2008)
U.S. v. Alvarez (2012)
Burwell v. Hobby Lobby (2015)

Civil Rights
Dred Scott v. Sanford (1857)
Plessy v. Ferguson (1893)
Brown v. Board of Education (1954)
Roe v. Wade (1973)
U.S. v. Virginia (1996)

Chapter 8. Public Opinion

Studying the Chapter Content

- ☐ Read the introductory paragraphs at the beginning of the chapter.
- ☐ Read the "Summary" paragraphs at the end of the chapter.
- ☐ Scan the chapter, noting the major headings and subheadings, and bolded vocabulary terms
- ☐ Take note of tables and figures in the chapter.
- ☐ Review the study questions in this guide for the chapter, and note how they correspond to the major sections of the chapter.
- ☐ Based on your survey of the major headings and subheadings of the chapter, generate a set of your own questions about the chapter.
- ☐ Read the chapter carefully in light of the study guide questions and the questions you have developed. Consider dividing your reading and study time into 2-3 subsections at a time.
- ☐ Outline the chapter, noting key concepts and the authors' conclusions.
- ☐ Review the study guide questions and your own study questions, attempting to address those questions in your own words.
- ☐ Make flashcards for the vocabulary terms and key concepts, and study them regularly.
- ☐ Review your notes as needed to prepare for the first assessment.
- ☐ Review your notes and the text as needed to prepare for subsequent assessments.

Chapter 8 Study Questions

1. How does "public opinion" pertain to the power problem? How do the two major models of democratic systems view public opinion? What are presidential approval ratings and what affects them? What does it mean to "wag the dog"?
2. What is "public opinion"? What is the Delegate Model? What is the Trustee Model? What were the Founders' intentions with regard to public opinion?
3. What are the primary agents of political socialization? How do they impact political socialization?
4. Can public opinion be changed by external forces? How is public opinion influenced by the political marketplace of ideas? How does the government try to influence that marketplace of ideas?
5. How does public opinion relate to the basic premises of democratic theory? How is public opinion measured? What are some important factors to take into account in evaluating public opinion gathering methods?
6. What were the strengths and weaknesses of public opinion polling in the 2016 election? Were the polls wrong?
7. What are some ways of comparing Americans' political opinions with those of other countries' citizens?

Key terms and concepts

Coverage bias	Political socialization	Response bias
Delegate model	Propaganda	Trustee model
Gender gap Marketplace of ideas	Public opinion	Wagging the dog
Nonresponse bias	Question wording bias	

Chapter 9. Political Ideology

Studying the Chapter Content

- ❏ Read the introductory paragraphs at the beginning of the chapter.
- ❏ Read the "Summary" paragraphs at the end of the chapter.
- ❏ Scan the chapter, noting the major headings and subheadings, and bolded vocabulary terms
- ❏ Take note of tables and figures in the chapter.
- ❏ Review the study questions in this guide for the chapter, and note how they correspond to the major sections of the chapter.
- ❏ Based on your survey of the major headings and subheadings of the chapter, generate a set of your own questions about the chapter.
- ❏ Read the chapter carefully in light of the study guide questions and the questions you have developed. Consider dividing your reading and study time into 2-3 subsections at a time.
- ❏ Outline the chapter, noting key concepts and the authors' conclusions.
- ❏ Review the study guide questions and your own study questions, attempting to address those questions in your own words.
- ❏ Make flashcards for the vocabulary terms and key concepts, and study them regularly.
- ❏ Review your notes as needed to prepare for the first assessment.
- ❏ Review your notes and the text as needed to prepare for subsequent assessments.

Chapter 9 Study Questions

1. What is an ideology? What makes a set of ideas an ideology? Why is its coherence important? What are the functions of an ideology?
2. What are the major issue areas that divide modern liberals and conservatives?
3. What are the main principles of conservatism? How has the ideology evolved such that modern conservatism is different from traditional conservatism?
4. What are the main principles of liberalism? How has the ideology evolved such that modern liberalism is different from traditional liberalism? What is the Harm Principle?
5. What are the main principles of libertarianism?
6. What are the main principles of socialism and communism? What are the main principles of anarchism? What are the main principles of populism? What are the main principles of feminism? What are the main principles of environmentalism? What are the main principles of fundamentalism? What are the main principles of terrorism? Why have there really only been two major ideologies in the US?
7. How does the text suggest we evaluate ideologies? How do prescriptive and descriptive ideas relate to ideologies?

Key terms and concepts

Anarchism
Communism
Conservatism, Traditional and Modern
Descriptive statement
Environmentalism
Feminism
Fundamentalism
Harm Principle
Ideology
Liberalism, Classical and Modern
Libertarianism
Prescriptive statement
Socialism
Terrorism

OpenStax American Government, Chapter 7. Voting and Elections

IMPORTANT NOTE: This study guide section is not from the Lenz and Holman textbook but from the OpenStax American Government text. The reading can be accessed at
https://cnx.org/contents/nY32AU8S@5.6:gRYwJb9C@9/Introduction

Studying the Chapter Content

- Read in the US Constitution: Article I Section 1, subsections 1-3; Article II Section 1, subsections 1-4; Article IV Section 4; Amendments XII, XV, XVII, XIX, XXIII, XXIV, XXVI.
- Read the introductory paragraphs at the beginning of the chapter.
- Read the "Summary" paragraphs at the end of the chapter.
- Scan the chapter, noting the major headings and subheadings, and bolded vocabulary terms
- Take note of tables and figures in the chapter.
- Review the study questions in this guide for the chapter, and note how they correspond to the major sections of the chapter.
- Based on your survey of the major headings and subheadings of the chapter, generate a set of your own questions about the chapter.
- Read the chapter carefully in light of the study guide questions and the questions you have developed. Consider dividing your reading and study time into 2-3 subsections at a time.
- Outline the chapter, noting key concepts and the authors' conclusions.
- Review the study guide questions and your own study questions, attempting to address those questions in your own words.
- Make flashcards for the vocabulary terms and key concepts, and study them regularly.
- Review your notes as needed to prepare for the first assessment.
- Review your notes and the text as needed to prepare for subsequent assessments.

OpenStax Chapter 7 Study Questions

1. Why do governments require people to register if they want to vote in elections? In what ways do states implement voter registration? Why is this sometimes a controversial process? How did the Voting Rights Act of 1965 affect states' voter registration processes? How and when does someone register to vote?
2. In what ways does voter turnout get measured? What factors are related to voter turnout? How do campaigns and civic groups attempt to change peoples' voting behavior? Which demographic groups are more likely to vote, and which are less likely to vote? Why do some groups favor actions like photo identification laws, while others oppose them?
3. What factors are related to peoples' decisions whether to run for political office? What is the basic purpose for campaign finance laws? What was the effect of the *Citizens United* case on campaign spending? If you wanted to contribute to a candidate in the 2015-16 elections, what is the most you could contribute to a candidate committee? What are the major methods for selecting party candidates, and what are the differences between them? What are some criticisms of these processes? What is the role of the parties'

political conventions? What is the time frame for the general election? How important are debates? What is the Electoral College, and how does it basically work? What are midterm elections?
4. Why is fundraising important in understanding elections? How do campaign strategies differ between primary and general election campaigns? What factors seem to matter the most in each type? How has campaign technology evolved? When citizens vote, how do they make their decisions? Why do incumbents have an advantage over challengers?
5. What are the different forms of direct democracy? What are the reasons states sometimes use direct democracy? What are the positives and negatives of direct democracy?

Key terms and concepts

Ballot fatigue	Political Action Committees (PACs)
Caucus	Primary (open, closed, top-two)
Coattail effect	Prospective voting
Competitive seat	Recall
Delegate	Referendum
Electoral College	Residency requirement
Incumbency advantage	Retrospective voting
Incumbent	Straight-ticket voting
Initiative	SuperPACs
Midterm election	Voting-age population
National Voter Registration Act (Motor Voter)	Voting-eligible population
Pocketbook voting	Voting Rights Act of 1965

Court Cases to Know

Citizens United v. Federal Election Commission (2010)
Shelby County v. Holder (2013)

Chapter 10. Political Participation

Studying the Chapter Content

- [ ] Read the introductory paragraphs at the beginning of the chapter.
- [ ] Read the "Summary" paragraphs at the end of the chapter.
- [ ] Scan the chapter, noting the major headings and subheadings, and bolded vocabulary terms
- [ ] Take note of tables and figures in the chapter.
- [ ] Review the study questions in this guide for the chapter, and note how they correspond to the major sections of the chapter.
- [ ] Based on your survey of the major headings and subheadings of the chapter, generate a set of your own questions about the chapter.
- [ ] Read the chapter carefully in light of the study guide questions and the questions you have developed. Consider dividing your reading and study time into 2-3 subsections at a time.
- [ ] Outline the chapter, noting key concepts and the authors' conclusions.
- [ ] Review the study guide questions and your own study questions, attempting to address those questions in your own words.
- [ ] Make flashcards for the vocabulary terms and key concepts, and study them regularly.
- [ ] Review your notes as needed to prepare for the first assessment.
- [ ] Review your notes and the text as needed to prepare for subsequent assessments.

Chapter 10 Study Questions

1. How does the power problem relate to political participation? What is *civic engagement*? In what ways have the right to vote been expanded and protected over US history? How is voting related to the question of "how" democratic the United States is? What kinds of factors help explain why some people vote and others don't? How do individual explanations contrast with system explanations?
2. What are the purposes of elections? What are *initiatives* and *referenda*? How are elections regulated? What is a primary election? What are the differences between the types of primary elections?
3. Which offices are elected through national elections? In what ways do presidential tickets get balanced? How does the Electoral College work? What are the main criticisms of the Electoral College? How frequently are congressional elections held? How often is each House seat up for reelection? How does *gerrymandering* affect elections?
4. What is an election *campaign*? Why are campaign messages important? [Money in campaigns was covered in OS Chapter 7, which we read earlier.] What is the campaign machine?
5. How do communications media affect campaigning? What is the relationship between campaign organizations and the media? How have social media and digital campaigning affected the campaign process? What is the role of fact-checking?
6. What are some effective approaches to civic engagement?

Key terms and concepts

Campaign	Individual explanations	Retail politics
Campaign machine	Political efficacy	System explanations

Caucus
Civic duty model
Civic engagement
Electoral College
Gerrymandering

Primaries, open and closed
Presidential primary
Rational choice model
Redistricting

Voter fatigue
Voter registration
Voter turnout
Wholesale politics

Chapter 11. Political Parties

Studying the Chapter Content

- ❏ Read the introductory paragraphs at the beginning of the chapter.
- ❏ Read the "Summary" paragraphs at the end of the chapter.
- ❏ Scan the chapter, noting the major headings and subheadings, and bolded vocabulary terms
- ❏ Take note of tables and figures in the chapter.
- ❏ Review the study questions in this guide for the chapter, and note how they correspond to the major sections of the chapter.
- ❏ Based on your survey of the major headings and subheadings of the chapter, generate a set of your own questions about the chapter.
- ❏ Read the chapter carefully in light of the study guide questions and the questions you have developed. Consider dividing your reading and study time into 2-3 subsections at a time.
- ❏ Outline the chapter, noting key concepts and the authors' conclusions.
- ❏ Review the study guide questions and your own study questions, attempting to address those questions in your own words.
- ❏ Make flashcards for the vocabulary terms and key concepts, and study them regularly.
- ❏ Review your notes as needed to prepare for the first assessment.
- ❏ Review your notes and the text as needed to prepare for subsequent assessments.

Chapter 11 Study Questions

1. In what two ways is the power problem related to the role of political parties in the American system? Why are political parties important linkage (mediating) institutions?
2. What are the roles of political parties in modern democracies?
3. How were political parties viewed during the founding generation? How does the constitution deal directly with political parties? Indirectly?
4. What are the characteristics of one-party systems? What are the characteristics of two-party systems? What are the characteristics of multi-party systems? Which best describes the US system? Why is the single member district plurality vote system important? Compare it with a proportional representation system. Why is it important to understand the rules of elections? In a two-party system how can a third or minor party be successful?
5. What are the two major political parties?
6. What were the major characteristics of and major parties during each of the political party eras? What are the major "legs" of the modern Republican party, and how do they contrast with the Democratic party?
7. How have major political and social movements interact with the political parties? What are the component groups of the modern Democratic and Republican party coalitions? How is the "just society" belief important for understanding Donald Trump's appeal? What are the major factors that political scientists use for explaining voting? How do views on race interact with these factors? How does party affiliation relate to political attitudes? How are US political parties affected by global economic and ideological trends? What is the election integrity movement, and how has it affected US politics? To what extent is there actual, documented, voter fraud in the US?

Key terms and concepts

- Anti-Federalist party
- Democrat/Democratic party
- Democratic Republican party
- Duverger's Law
- Election integrity
- Election fraud
- Federalist party
- Ins and Outs
- Jacksonian Democracy
- Just society belief
- Linkage institution
- Party identification
- Party system
- Plurality vote system
- Political party
- Proportional representation
- Republican party
- Single member district system
- Washington's Farewell Address
- Whig party
- Winner-take-all system

Chapter 12. Interest Groups

Studying the Chapter Content

- ☐ Read the introductory paragraphs at the beginning of the chapter.
- ☐ Read the "Summary" paragraphs at the end of the chapter.
- ☐ Scan the chapter, noting the major headings and subheadings, and bolded vocabulary terms
- ☐ Take note of tables and figures in the chapter.
- ☐ Review the study questions in this guide for the chapter, and note how they correspond to the major sections of the chapter.
- ☐ Based on your survey of the major headings and subheadings of the chapter, generate a set of your own questions about the chapter.
- ☐ Read the chapter carefully in light of the study guide questions and the questions you have developed. Consider dividing your reading and study time into 2-3 subsections at a time.
- ☐ Outline the chapter, noting key concepts and the authors' conclusions.
- ☐ Review the study guide questions and your own study questions, attempting to address those questions in your own words.
- ☐ Make flashcards for the vocabulary terms and key concepts, and study them regularly.
- ☐ Review your notes as needed to prepare for the first assessment.
- ☐ Review your notes and the text as needed to prepare for subsequent assessments.

Chapter 12 Study Questions

1. What are the main differences between interest and interest group and a political party? What are the major types of interest groups, and what are they trying to accomplish?
2. Why do people join interest groups?
3. What are the main activities interest groups engage in? In what ways do they lobby Congress, the Executive Branch, and the courts? What are the basic relationships in an issue network? How does grassroots lobbying work? In what ways are interest groups involved in campaigns and elections? What other activities do interest group do?
4. What does it mean for an interest group to play "offense" or "defense"?
5. What is the Free Rider Problem? How does it complicate interest group activities?
6. What are the positives and negatives of interest groups in the American political system?

Key terms and concepts

Economic interest group
Free Rider Problem
Grassroots lobbying
Ideological Interest group
Interest group
Issue network

Lobbying
Material incentives
Political Action Committee (PAC)
Private good
Private interest group

Public good
Public interest group
Purposive incentives
Solidary incentives
Think tank

Chapter 7. The Media, Politics, and Government

Studying the Chapter Content

- Read the introductory paragraphs at the beginning of the chapter.
- Read the "Summary" paragraphs at the end of the chapter.
- Scan the chapter, noting the major headings and subheadings, and bolded vocabulary terms
- Take note of tables and figures in the chapter.
- Review the study questions in this guide for the chapter, and note how they correspond to the major sections of the chapter.
- Based on your survey of the major headings and subheadings of the chapter, generate a set of your own questions about the chapter.
- Read the chapter carefully in light of the study guide questions and the questions you have developed. Consider dividing your reading and study time into 2-3 subsections at a time.
- Outline the chapter, noting key concepts and the authors' conclusions.
- Review the study guide questions and your own study questions, attempting to address those questions in your own words.
- Make flashcards for the vocabulary terms and key concepts, and study them regularly.
- Review your notes as needed to prepare for the first assessment.
- Review your notes and the text as needed to prepare for subsequent assessments.

Chapter 7 Study Questions

1. What are the four main roles of the media in the United States?
2. What is the power problem as it relates to the media? What are the possible sources of bias in the media? Why does the text say there is a "love-hate" relationship between Americans and the press? What was the press like in the Founding Era? How is it different from the press in the modern era?
3. Compare mass, new, and social media. How has confidence in the press changed over the years? How has the rise of social media affected traditional media?
4. What is the relationship between the media and the political system? How does the media cover political news?
5. What are the major protections, limitations, and laws regulating expression in the media? What is the role of the Federal Communications Commission? What was the Fairness Doctrine, why did it get changed, and what have been the effects of that change?
6. How and why have people sought to re-regulate the mass media?
7. How do the authors evaluate the direction of media's role in politics?

Key terms and concepts

Bias	Framing	Professional press
Economic role	Libel laws	Social media
Educative role	Mass media	Socialization role
Fairness doctrine	Moral regulatory policy	Watchdog role
Federal Communications Commission	New media	Yellow journalism

Chapter 3. Congress

Studying the Chapter Content

- ☐ Read in the US Constitution Article I; Article IV Sections 3-4, and Amendments XVI, XVII, XX, XXVII.
- ☐ Read the introductory paragraphs at the beginning of the chapter.
- ☐ Read the "Summary" paragraphs at the end of the chapter.
- ☐ Scan the chapter, noting the major headings and subheadings, and bolded vocabulary terms
- ☐ Take note of tables and figures in the chapter.
- ☐ Review the study questions in this guide for the chapter, and note how they correspond to the major sections of the chapter.
- ☐ Based on your survey of the major headings and subheadings of the chapter, generate a set of your own questions about the chapter.
- ☐ Read the chapter carefully in light of the study guide questions and the questions you have developed. Consider dividing your reading and study time into 2-3 subsections at a time.
- ☐ Outline the chapter, noting key concepts and the authors' conclusions.
- ☐ Review the study guide questions and your own study questions, attempting to address those questions in your own words.
- ☐ Make flashcards for the vocabulary terms and key concepts, and study them regularly.
- ☐ Review your notes as needed to prepare for the first assessment.
- ☐ Review your notes and the text as needed to prepare for subsequent assessments.

Chapter 3 Study Questions

1. How does the power problem relate to Congress? Why is Congress called the "broken branch"? How has confidence in Congress changed over the years?
2. How did the founders envision the role for Congress? What was supposed to be its relation to the other branches of government? Why has Congress lost power relative to the Executive branch?
3. Is the concept of separation of powers absolute? What are some examples of how it isn't?
4. What are the two major categories of constitutional powers held by Congress?
5. What are the four main roles or functions of Congress? What are the three major theories of representation? How are they different? Why is constituency service important? What are the oversight functions of Congress? What are the roles of different types of hearings in congressional oversight?
6. How is Congress organized? Why are committees important? What are the different types of committees and how do they differ? What is the role of the Special Counsel? How are the political parties organized in the House and Senate? Who are the main leaders in the House and Senate? What is the basic process by which a bill becomes a law?

Key terms and concepts

Appropriations
Bicameralism
Conference committee

Joint committees
Legislation
Majority party

Representation
Select or special committees

Constituent
Constituency service
Delegate
Enumerated powers
Impeachment
Implied powers

Minority party
Necessary and proper clause
Oversight
Politico
President pro tempore

Speaker of the House
Standing committees
Trustee
Whip

Chapter 4. The Presidency

Studying the Chapter Content

- Read in the US Constitution Article II, and Amendments XX, XXII, and XXV.
- Read the introductory paragraphs at the beginning of the chapter.
- Read the "Summary" paragraphs at the end of the chapter.
- Scan the chapter, noting the major headings and subheadings, and bolded vocabulary terms
- Take note of tables and figures in the chapter.
- Review the study questions in this guide for the chapter, and note how they correspond to the major sections of the chapter.
- Based on your survey of the major headings and subheadings of the chapter, generate a set of your own questions about the chapter.
- Read the chapter carefully in light of the study guide questions and the questions you have developed. Consider dividing your reading and study time into 2-3 subsections at a time.
- Outline the chapter, noting key concepts and the authors' conclusions.
- Review the study guide questions and your own study questions, attempting to address those questions in your own words.
- Make flashcards for the vocabulary terms and key concepts, and study them regularly.
- Review your notes as needed to prepare for the first assessment.
- Review your notes and the text as needed to prepare for subsequent assessments.

Chapter 4 Study Questions

1. What is the difference between the president as a person and the presidency as an office? What is meant by the "unprecedented" president? What is meant by the "personal" presidency? What is meant by the "post-modern" presidency? How does viewing the presidency though the lens of popular culture help us understand the office? How does framing theory apply to the presidency? How does professional wrestling help us understand the modern presidency?
2. What is the power problem as it relates to the presidency? How has the power of the presidency changed compared to what the Founders envisioned? What are the formal constitutional powers of the president? What are the informal powers of the president?
3. What are the president's constitutionally enumerated and implied powers? What are the major statutes affecting the president's power? How have case law sources affected the president's power?
4. What are the political sources of a president's power? What makes presidents the leader of their respective political parties? Why does this matter? How do a president's personal political skills affect the president's power? How is a president's power affected by circumstances and events? How do events affect the president's approval rate? How is public opinion a source of political power for the president? What are the main dynamics of the relationship between the media and the president? How does this relationship affect and reflect the president's power?
5. How is the executive branch of the US government organized? Why did the Founders create the president the way they did?
6. What are the main constitutional requirements for being eligible to be president? What are the informal requirements? What is the main mechanism for electing the president?

What does the text mean when it asserts that Donald Trump "works the refs" in politics? How have expectations about the president being articulate and well-spoken changed over the years? What is the basic way the Electoral College works? What ar the arguments for and against the Electoral College in the modern era?
7. What is the bureaucracy? What are the main characteristics of a bureaucracy? How are executive departments organized? Who, if anyone, controls the bureaucracy? Why does the bureaucracy need to be controlled?

Key terms and concepts

Bureaucracy	Executive orders	Implied powers
Cabinet	Executive privilege	Informal powers
Electoral College	Framing theory	Personal presidency
Executive agreements	Imperial presidency	Post-modern presidency
Executive branch	Imperiled presidency	Sole organ doctrine
Executive Office of the President		

Key Laws and Cases to know

Employment Act of 1946
Authorization for the Use of Military Force in Afghanistan and Iraq (2002)
U.S. v. Curtiss-Wright (1936)

Chapter 5. The Courts

Studying the Chapter Content

- ❏ Read in the US Constitution Article III and Amendment XI.
- ❏ Read the introductory paragraphs at the beginning of the chapter.
- ❏ Read the "Summary" paragraphs at the end of the chapter.
- ❏ Scan the chapter, noting the major headings and subheadings, and bolded vocabulary terms
- ❏ Take note of tables and figures in the chapter.
- ❏ Review the study questions in this guide for the chapter, and note how they correspond to the major sections of the chapter.
- ❏ Based on your survey of the major headings and subheadings of the chapter, generate a set of your own questions about the chapter.
- ❏ Read the chapter carefully in light of the study guide questions and the questions you have developed. Consider dividing your reading and study time into 2-3 subsections at a time.
- ❏ Outline the chapter, noting key concepts and the authors' conclusions.
- ❏ Review the study guide questions and your own study questions, attempting to address those questions in your own words.
- ❏ Make flashcards for the vocabulary terms and key concepts, and study them regularly.
- ❏ Review your notes as needed to prepare for the first assessment.
- ❏ Review your notes and the text as needed to prepare for subsequent assessments.

Chapter 5 Study Questions

1. What is the power problem as it relates to the federal court system?
2. What have been the major eras in the history of the Supreme Court? What were the major controversies in each era?
3. How powerful is the judicial branch of the government compared to the other branches? How has this power fluctuated over time? What is *judicial review*, and why is it important? What are the limits on judicial power?
4. What are the two main functions of courts? How is the courts system set up to accomplish these functions? How are the federal courts organized? What are the main types of US Supreme Court jurisdiction?
5. What is the process by which federal judges are selected? What are the important factors that go into this selection? What is the role of the Senate in this process? What does the text mean when it refers to Republicans "playing hardball" with judicial selection?
6. In what ways does the law inform court decisions? In what ways does politics inform court decisions? Compare the *Classical/Legal* and *Legal Realist/Political* models of judicial decision-making. Compare the *Crime Control* and *Due Process* models of justice.
7. What is the role of juries in implementing justice? What is the role of trials in the criminal justice system? What are the key factors involved in determining the facts of criminal cases? In what ways have the courts sought to limit racial bias in justice administration? To what have they been successful?

Key terms and concepts

- Court packing plan
- Culture wars
- Dispute resolution
- Federalist #78
- Framers' intentions
- Jurisdiction
- Law interpretation
- Judicial activism
- Judicial restraint
- Judicial review
- *Marbury vs. Madison* (1803)
- John Marshall
- Plain meaning
- Precedent

Chapter 13. Public Policy

Studying the Chapter Content

- ❑ Read the introductory paragraphs at the beginning of the chapter.
- ❑ Read the "Summary" paragraphs at the end of the chapter.
- ❑ Scan the chapter, noting the major headings and subheadings, and bolded vocabulary terms
- ❑ Take note of tables and figures in the chapter.
- ❑ Review the study questions in this guide for the chapter, and note how they correspond to the major sections of the chapter.
- ❑ Based on your survey of the major headings and subheadings of the chapter, generate a set of your own questions about the chapter.
- ❑ Read the chapter carefully in light of the study guide questions and the questions you have developed. Consider dividing your reading and study time into 2-3 subsections at a time.
- ❑ Outline the chapter, noting key concepts and the authors' conclusions.
- ❑ Review the study guide questions and your own study questions, attempting to address those questions in your own words.
- ❑ Make flashcards for the vocabulary terms and key concepts, and study them regularly.
- ❑ Review your notes as needed to prepare for the first assessment.
- ❑ Review your notes and the text as needed to prepare for subsequent assessments.

Chapter 13 Study Questions

1. What is policy? What differentiates policy from public policy?
2. What is involved in the agenda setting stage in the policy making process? What is involved in this stage? How do the examples provided in the book illuminate aspects of this stage?
3. What is involved in the policy formulation stage in the policy making process? What is involved in the policy adoption stage in the policy making process? What is involved in the implementation stage in the policy making process? What is involved in budgeting? What is involved in the evaluation stage in the policy making process? Why is it useful to study unintended results of policies? What are the differences between distributive policies and regulatory policies? How is social policy both distributive and regulatory?
4. How is health care policy illustrative of the overall policy making process?
5. How is environmental policy, including the "water wars" and climate change policy, illustrative of the overall policy making process?
6. How is energy policy illustrative of the overall policy making process?
7. How is immigration policy illustrative of the overall policy making process? How are views of demography important in this process? How are the economy and views of American political destiny important in this process? What is the *Age Dependency Ratio* and how is it related to immigration policy? How does the concept of entitlement relate to policy making in general? Why does the book argue that the labor force participation rate is a more meaningful measure of economic performance than the unemployment rate?

Key terms and concepts

Agenda setting	Immigration policy	Policy implementation
Age dependency ratio	Labor force participation rate	Public policy
Budgeting	Policy	Regulatory policy
Climate change	Policy adoption	Social policy
Distributive policy	Policy evaluation	Unemployment rate
Entitlement		